Gratitude for teens:

with prompts

Is a book to help you remember all the
things you are grateful for. Each page
has prompts to help you remember
whatever made you happy that day.
Being grateful helps you to feel yes I
can do this!! Gratitude helps you to
feel positive and notice what you have.
It helps you feel happier!!

Its 6" x 9" in dimension and has 123
pages in the book.

Gratitude for teens:

with prompts

I hope this journal helps you on your journey.

Thank you for buying this book.

ISBN: 9781096092230

lavenderbluebooks@gmail.com

Date: ☼

Quote Of The Day
_____
_____
_____

Today I am truly grateful for...
_____
_____
_____
_____
_____

Here's what would make today great...
_____
_____
_____
_____

I am...
_____
_____
_____

Some amazing things that happened today...
_____
_____

Some amazing things that happened today...
_____
_____

What could I have done to make today even better?
_____
_____

Date: _____

Quote Of The Day

_____

_____

_____

Today I am truly grateful for...

_____

_____

_____

_____

_____

Here's what would make today great...

_____

_____

_____

_____

I am...

_____

_____

_____

Some amazing things that happened today...

_____

_____

Some amazing things that happened today...

_____

_____

_____

What could I have done to make today even better?

_____

_____

Date: _____

Quote Of The Day

_____

_____

Today I am truly grateful for...

_____

_____

_____

_____

Here's what would make today great...

_____

_____

_____

_____

I am...

_____

_____

_____

Some amazing things that happened today...

_____

_____

Some amazing things that happened today...

_____

_____

What could I have done to make today even better?

_____

Date: _____

Quote Of The Day

_____

_____

_____

Today I am truly grateful for...

_____

_____

_____

_____

_____

Here's what would make today great...

_____

_____

_____

_____

I am...

_____

_____

_____

Some amazing things that happened today...

_____

_____

Some amazing things that happened today...

_____

_____

_____

What could I have done to make today even better?

_____

_____

Date: _____

Quote Of The Day

_____
_____
_____

Today I am truly grateful for...

_____
_____
_____
_____
_____

Here's what would make today great...

_____
_____
_____
_____
_____

I am...

_____
_____
_____

Some amazing things that happened today...

_____
_____

Some amazing things that happened today...

_____
_____

What could I have done to make today even better?

_____
_____

Date:

Quote Of The Day

_____

_____

_____

Today I am truly grateful for...

_____

_____

_____

_____

_____

Here's what would make today great...

_____

_____

_____

_____

_____

I am...

_____

_____

_____

Some amazing things that happened today...

_____

_____

Some amazing things that happened today...

_____

_____

What could I have done to make today even better?

_____

_____

Date:

Quote Of The Day

_____

_____

_____

Today I am truly grateful for...

_____

_____

_____

_____

_____

Here's what would make today great...

_____

_____

_____

_____

I am...

_____

_____

_____

Some amazing things that happened today...

_____

_____

Some amazing things that happened today...

_____

_____

What could I have done to make today even better?

_____

_____

Date: _____

Quote Of The Day

_____

_____

_____

Today I am truly grateful for...

_____

_____

_____

_____

_____

Here's what would make today great...

_____

_____

_____

_____

I am...

_____

_____

_____

Some amazing things that happened today...

_____

_____

Some amazing things that happened today...

_____

_____

What could I have done to make today even better?

_____

_____

Date:

Quote Of The Day

_____

_____

Today I am truly grateful for...

_____

_____

_____

_____

Here's what would make today great...

_____

_____

_____

_____

I am...

_____

_____

_____

Some amazing things that happened today...

_____

_____

Some amazing things that happened today...

_____

_____

What could I have done to make today even better?

_____

Date: _____

Quote Of The Day

_____

_____

_____

Today I am truly grateful for...

_____

_____

_____

_____

_____

Here's what would make today great...

_____

_____

_____

_____

_____

I am...

_____

_____

_____

Some amazing things that happened today...

_____

_____

Some amazing things that happened today...

_____

_____

_____

What could I have done to make today even better?

_____

_____

Date: _____

☀

Quote Of The Day

_____
_____
_____

Today I am truly grateful for...

_____
_____
_____
_____
_____

Here's what would make today great...

_____
_____
_____
_____

I am...

_____
_____
_____

Some amazing things that happened today...

_____
_____

Some amazing things that happened today...

_____
_____

What could I have done to make today even better?

_____
_____

Date: _____

Quote Of The Day

_____
_____
_____

Today I am truly grateful for...

_____
_____
_____
_____
_____
_____

Here's what would make today great...

_____
_____
_____
_____
_____
_____

I am...

_____
_____
_____

Some amazing things that happened today...

_____
_____

Some amazing things that happened today...

_____
_____

What could I have done to make today even better?

_____
_____

Date:

Quote Of The Day

_____

_____

Today I am truly grateful for...

_____

_____

_____

_____

Here's what would make today great...

_____

_____

_____

_____

I am...

_____

_____

Some amazing things that happened today...

_____

_____

Some amazing things that happened today...

_____

_____

What could I have done to make today even better?

_____

Date: _____

Quote Of The Day

_____

_____

_____

Today I am truly grateful for...

_____

_____

_____

_____

Here's what would make today great...

_____

_____

_____

_____

I am...

_____

_____

_____

Some amazing things that happened today...

_____

_____

Some amazing things that happened today...

_____

_____

What could I have done to make today even better?

_____

_____

Date:

Quote Of The Day

_____

_____

Today I am truly grateful for...

_____

_____

_____

_____

Here's what would make today great...

_____

_____

_____

_____

I am...

_____

_____

Some amazing things that happened today...

_____

_____

Some amazing things that happened today...

_____

_____

What could I have done to make today even better?

_____

Date: _____

Quote Of The Day

_____

_____

_____

Today I am truly grateful for...

_____

_____

_____

_____

_____

Here's what would make today great...

_____

_____

_____

_____

I am...

_____

_____

_____

Some amazing things that happened today...

_____

_____

Some amazing things that happened today...

_____

_____

What could I have done to make today even better?

_____

_____

Date: ☀

Quote Of The Day

_____

_____

_____

Today I am truly grateful for...

_____

_____

_____

_____

_____

Here's what would make today great...

_____

_____

_____

_____

I am...

_____

_____

_____

Some amazing things that happened today...

_____

_____

Some amazing things that happened today... ✨ ✨ 🌙

_____

_____

What could I have done to make today even better?

_____

_____

Date:

Quote Of The Day

Today I am truly grateful for...

Here's what would make today great...

I am...

Some amazing things that happened today...

Some amazing things that happened today...

What could I have done to make today even better?

Date: ☼

Quote Of The Day

_____

_____

Today I am truly grateful for...

_____

_____

_____

_____

Here's what would make today great...

_____

_____

_____

_____

I am...

_____

_____

Some amazing things that happened today...

_____

_____

Some amazing things that happened today...

_____

_____

What could I have done to make today even better?

_____

Date: _____

Quote Of The Day
_____
_____
_____

Today I am truly grateful for...
_____
_____
_____
_____
_____

Here's what would make today great...
_____
_____
_____
_____
_____

I am...
_____
_____
_____

Some amazing things that happened today...
_____
_____

Some amazing things that happened today...
_____
_____

What could I have done to make today even better?
_____
_____

Date:

Quote Of The Day

_____

Today I am truly grateful for...

_____

Here's what would make today great...

_____

I am...

_____

Some amazing things that happened today...

_____

Some amazing things that happened today...

_____

What could I have done to make today even better?

_____

Date: _____

Quote Of The Day

_____

_____

_____

Today I am truly grateful for...

_____

_____

_____

_____

_____

Here's what would make today great...

_____

_____

_____

_____

_____

I am...

_____

_____

_____

Some amazing things that happened today...

_____

_____

Some amazing things that happened today...

_____

_____

_____

What could I have done to make today even better?

_____

_____

Date: _____

Quote Of The Day

_____

_____

Today I am truly grateful for...

_____

_____

_____

_____

Here's what would make today great...

_____

_____

_____

I am...

_____

_____

Some amazing things that happened today...

_____

_____

Some amazing things that happened today...

_____

_____

What could I have done to make today even better?

_____

_____

Date:

Quote Of The Day

_____

_____

Today I am truly grateful for...

_____

_____

_____

_____

_____

Here's what would make today great...

_____

_____

_____

_____

_____

I am...

_____

_____

_____

Some amazing things that happened today...

_____

_____

Some amazing things that happened today...

_____

_____

What could I have done to make today even better?

_____

_____

Date: _____

☀

Quote Of The Day
_____
_____

Today I am truly grateful for...
_____
_____
_____
_____
_____

Here's what would make today great...
_____
_____
_____
_____

I am...
_____
_____
_____

Some amazing things that happened today...
_____
_____

Some amazing things that happened today...

✨ ✨ 🌙

_____
_____

What could I have done to make today even better?
_____
_____

Date: _____

Quote Of The Day

_____

_____

_____

Today I am truly grateful for...

_____

_____

_____

_____

_____

Here's what would make today great...

_____

_____

_____

_____

I am...

_____

_____

_____

Some amazing things that happened today...

_____

_____

Some amazing things that happened today...

_____

_____

_____

What could I have done to make today even better?

_____

_____

Date:

Quote Of The Day

_____

_____

Today I am truly grateful for...

_____

_____

_____

_____

_____

Here's what would make today great...

_____

_____

_____

_____

I am...

_____

_____

Some amazing things that happened today...

_____

_____

Some amazing things that happened today...

_____

_____

What could I have done to make today even better?

_____

_____

Date: _____

Quote Of The Day

_____

_____

_____

Today I am truly grateful for...

_____

_____

_____

_____

_____

Here's what would make today great...

_____

_____

_____

_____

I am...

_____

_____

_____

Some amazing things that happened today...

_____

_____

Some amazing things that happened today...

_____

_____

What could I have done to make today even better?

_____

_____

Date:

☀

Quote Of The Day

_____

_____

_____

Today I am truly grateful for...

_____

_____

_____

_____

_____

Here's what would make today great...

_____

_____

_____

_____

_____

I am...

_____

_____

_____

Some amazing things that happened today...

_____

_____

Some amazing things that happened today...

_____

_____

What could I have done to make today even better?

_____

_____

Date: _____

Quote Of The Day

_____

_____

_____

Today I am truly grateful for...

_____

_____

_____

_____

_____

Here's what would make today great...

_____

_____

_____

_____

_____

I am...

_____

_____

_____

Some amazing things that happened today...

_____

_____

_____

Some amazing things that happened today...

_____

_____

_____

What could I have done to make today even better?

_____

_____

Date:

Quote Of The Day

_____

_____

Today I am truly grateful for...

_____

_____

_____

_____

Here's what would make today great...

_____

_____

_____

_____

I am...

_____

_____

_____

Some amazing things that happened today...

_____

_____

Some amazing things that happened today...

_____

_____

What could I have done to make today even better?

_____

_____

Date:

Quote Of The Day

_____

Today I am truly grateful for...

_____

_____

_____

Here's what would make today great...

_____

_____

_____

I am...

_____

_____

Some amazing things that happened today...

_____

Some amazing things that happened today...

_____

What could I have done to make today even better?

_____

Date:

Quote Of The Day

_____

_____

Today I am truly grateful for...

_____

_____

_____

_____

Here's what would make today great...

_____

_____

_____

_____

I am...

_____

_____

_____

Some amazing things that happened today...

_____

_____

Some amazing things that happened today...

_____

_____

What could I have done to make today even better?

_____

_____

Date: _____

Quote Of The Day

_____
_____
_____

Today I am truly grateful for...

_____
_____
_____
_____
_____

Here's what would make today great...

_____
_____
_____
_____

I am...

_____
_____
_____

Some amazing things that happened today...

_____
_____

Some amazing things that happened today...

_____
_____

What could I have done to make today even better?

_____
_____

Date: _____

☀

Quote Of The Day
_____
_____
_____

Today I am truly grateful for...
_____
_____
_____
_____
_____

Here's what would make today great...
_____
_____
_____
_____

I am...
_____
_____
_____

Some amazing things that happened today...
_____
_____

Some amazing things that happened today...

✦ ✦ ✦ ☽
_____
_____

What could I have done to make today even better?
_____
_____

Date: _____

Quote Of The Day

_____
_____

Today I am truly grateful for...

_____
_____
_____
_____

Here's what would make today great...

_____
_____
_____
_____

I am...

_____
_____

Some amazing things that happened today...

_____
_____

Some amazing things that happened today...

_____
_____

What could I have done to make today even better?

_____

Date: _____

Quote Of The Day

_____
_____
_____

Today I am truly grateful for...

_____
_____
_____
_____
_____

Here's what would make today great...

_____
_____
_____
_____

I am...

_____
_____
_____

Some amazing things that happened today...

_____
_____

Some amazing things that happened today...

_____
_____
_____

What could I have done to make today even better?

_____

Date:

Quote Of The Day

Today I am truly grateful for...

Here's what would make today great...

I am...

Some amazing things that happened today...

Some amazing things that happened today...

What could I have done to make today even better?

Date:

Quote Of The Day

_____

_____

_____

Today I am truly grateful for...

_____

_____

_____

_____

_____

Here's what would make today great...

_____

_____

_____

_____

I am...

_____

_____

_____

Some amazing things that happened today...

_____

_____

Some amazing things that happened today...

_____

_____

What could I have done to make today even better?

_____

Date: _____

Quote Of The Day
_____
_____
_____

Today I am truly grateful for...
_____
_____
_____
_____
_____

Here's what would make today great...
_____
_____
_____
_____
_____

I am...
_____
_____
_____

Some amazing things that happened today...
_____
_____

Some amazing things that happened today...
_____
_____

What could I have done to make today even better?
_____
_____

Date: _____

☀

Quote Of The Day

_____

_____

_____

Today I am truly grateful for...

_____

_____

_____

_____

_____

Here's what would make today great...

_____

_____

_____

_____

_____

I am...

_____

_____

_____

Some amazing things that happened today...

_____

_____

Some amazing things that happened today...

✦ ✦ ☽

_____

_____

What could I have done to make today even better?

_____

_____

Date: _____

Quote Of The Day

_____
_____
_____

Today I am truly grateful for...

_____
_____
_____
_____
_____

Here's what would make today great...

_____
_____
_____
_____
_____

I am...

_____
_____
_____

Some amazing things that happened today...

_____
_____

Some amazing things that happened today...

_____
_____

What could I have done to make today even better?

_____
_____

Date: _____

Quote Of The Day

_____

_____

Today I am truly grateful for...

_____

_____

_____

_____

Here's what would make today great...

_____

_____

_____

_____

I am...

_____

_____

Some amazing things that happened today...

_____

_____

Some amazing things that happened today...

_____

_____

What could I have done to make today even better?

_____

_____

Date: _____

☀

Quote Of The Day

_____
_____
_____

Today I am truly grateful for...

_____
_____
_____
_____
_____

Here's what would make today great...

_____
_____
_____
_____

I am...

_____
_____
_____

Some amazing things that happened today...

_____
_____

Some amazing things that happened today...

_____
_____

What could I have done to make today even better?

_____
_____

Date: _____

Quote Of The Day

_____

_____

Today I am truly grateful for...

_____

_____

_____

_____

Here's what would make today great...

_____

_____

_____

_____

I am...

_____

_____

_____

Some amazing things that happened today...

_____

_____

Some amazing things that happened today...

_____

_____

What could I have done to make today even better?

_____

Date: _____

Quote Of The Day

_____
_____
_____

Today I am truly grateful for...

_____
_____
_____
_____
_____

Here's what would make today great...

_____
_____
_____
_____
_____

I am...

_____
_____
_____

Some amazing things that happened today...

_____
_____

Some amazing things that happened today...

_____
_____
_____

What could I have done to make today even better?

_____
_____

Date:

☀

Quote Of The Day
_____
_____

Today I am truly grateful for...
_____
_____
_____
_____
_____

Here's what would make today great...
_____
_____
_____
_____
_____

I am...
_____
_____
_____

Some amazing things that happened today...
_____
_____

Some amazing things that happened today...   ✦ ✦ 🌙
_____
_____
_____

What could I have done to make today even better?
_____
_____

Date: _____

Quote Of The Day
_____
_____
_____

Today I am truly grateful for...
_____
_____
_____
_____
_____

Here's what would make today great...
_____
_____
_____
_____
_____

I am...
_____
_____
_____

Some amazing things that happened today...
_____
_____

Some amazing things that happened today...
_____
_____

What could I have done to make today even better?
_____
_____

Date: _____

Quote Of The Day

_____

_____

Today I am truly grateful for...

_____

_____

_____

_____

Here's what would make today great...

_____

_____

_____

_____

I am...

_____

_____

Some amazing things that happened today...

_____

_____

Some amazing things that happened today...

_____

_____

What could I have done to make today even better?

_____

_____

Date:

Quote Of The Day

_____

Today I am truly grateful for...

_____

Here's what would make today great...

_____

I am...

_____

Some amazing things that happened today...

_____

Some amazing things that happened today...

_____

What could I have done to make today even better?

_____

Date: _____

Quote Of The Day

_____

_____

Today I am truly grateful for...

_____

_____

_____

_____

Here's what would make today great...

_____

_____

_____

_____

I am...

_____

_____

_____

Some amazing things that happened today...

_____

_____

Some amazing things that happened today...

_____

_____

What could I have done to make today even better?

_____

_____

Date: _____

Quote Of The Day

_____

_____

_____

Today I am truly grateful for...

_____

_____

_____

_____

Here's what would make today great...

_____

_____

_____

_____

I am...

_____

_____

_____

Some amazing things that happened today...

_____

_____

Some amazing things that happened today...

_____

_____

What could I have done to make today even better?

_____

_____

Date:

Quote Of The Day

_____

_____

_____

Today I am truly grateful for...

_____

_____

_____

_____

_____

Here's what would make today great...

_____

_____

_____

_____

_____

I am...

_____

_____

_____

Some amazing things that happened today...

_____

_____

_____

Some amazing things that happened today...

_____

_____

_____

What could I have done to make today even better?

_____

_____

Date:

Quote Of The Day

_____

_____

Today I am truly grateful for...

_____

_____

_____

_____

Here's what would make today great...

_____

_____

_____

_____

I am...

_____

_____

_____

Some amazing things that happened today...

_____

_____

Some amazing things that happened today...

_____

_____

What could I have done to make today even better?

_____

_____

Date:

Quote Of The Day

_____

_____

Today I am truly grateful for...

_____

_____

_____

_____

Here's what would make today great...

_____

_____

_____

I am...

_____

_____

Some amazing things that happened today...

_____

_____

Some amazing things that happened today...

_____

_____

What could I have done to make today even better?

_____

_____

Date: _____

Quote Of The Day

_____

_____

_____

Today I am truly grateful for...

_____

_____

_____

_____

_____

Here's what would make today great...

_____

_____

_____

_____

I am...

_____

_____

_____

Some amazing things that happened today...

_____

_____

Some amazing things that happened today...

_____

_____

_____

What could I have done to make today even better?

_____

_____

Date:

Quote Of The Day

_____

_____

Today I am truly grateful for...

_____

_____

_____

_____

Here's what would make today great...

_____

_____

_____

_____

I am...

_____

_____

_____

Some amazing things that happened today...

_____

_____

Some amazing things that happened today...

_____

_____

What could I have done to make today even better?

_____

_____

Date: _____

Quote Of The Day
_____
_____
_____

Today I am truly grateful for...
_____
_____
_____
_____
_____

Here's what would make today great...
_____
_____
_____
_____

I am...
_____
_____
_____

Some amazing things that happened today...
_____
_____

Some amazing things that happened today...
_____
_____

What could I have done to make today even better?
_____
_____

Date: _____

Quote Of The Day

_____

_____

Today I am truly grateful for...

_____

_____

_____

_____

Here's what would make today great...

_____

_____

_____

_____

I am...

_____

_____

Some amazing things that happened today...

_____

_____

Some amazing things that happened today...

_____

_____

What could I have done to make today even better?

_____

_____

Date:

Quote Of The Day

_____

_____

_____

Today I am truly grateful for...

_____

_____

_____

_____

_____

Here's what would make today great...

_____

_____

_____

_____

_____

I am...

_____

_____

_____

Some amazing things that happened today...

_____

_____

Some amazing things that happened today...

_____

_____

What could I have done to make today even better?

_____

_____

Date:

Quote Of The Day

_____

Today I am truly grateful for...

_____

Here's what would make today great...

_____

I am...

_____

Some amazing things that happened today...

_____

Some amazing things that happened today...

_____

What could I have done to make today even better?

_____

Date: _____

Quote Of The Day

_____
_____
_____

Today I am truly grateful for...

_____
_____
_____
_____
_____

Here's what would make today great...

_____
_____
_____
_____
_____

I am...

_____
_____
_____

Some amazing things that happened today...

_____
_____

Some amazing things that happened today...

_____
_____

What could I have done to make today even better?

_____
_____

Date:

Quote Of The Day

_____

_____

Today I am truly grateful for...

_____

_____

_____

_____

Here's what would make today great...

_____

_____

_____

_____

I am...

_____

_____

_____

Some amazing things that happened today...

_____

_____

Some amazing things that happened today...

_____

_____

What could I have done to make today even better?

_____

_____

Date:

Quote Of The Day

_____

_____

_____

Today I am truly grateful for...

_____

_____

_____

_____

_____

Here's what would make today great...

_____

_____

_____

_____

I am...

_____

_____

_____

Some amazing things that happened today...

_____

_____

Some amazing things that happened today...

_____

_____

What could I have done to make today even better?

_____

_____

Date: _____

Quote Of The Day

_____

_____

Today I am truly grateful for...

_____

_____

_____

_____

Here's what would make today great...

_____

_____

_____

_____

I am...

_____

_____

Some amazing things that happened today...

_____

_____

Some amazing things that happened today...

_____

_____

What could I have done to make today even better?

_____

_____

Date:

Quote Of The Day

Today I am truly grateful for...

Here's what would make today great...

I am...

Some amazing things that happened today...

Some amazing things that happened today...

What could I have done to make today even better?

Date:

Quote Of The Day

_____

_____

Today I am truly grateful for...

_____

_____

_____

_____

Here's what would make today great...

_____

_____

_____

_____

I am...

_____

_____

_____

Some amazing things that happened today...

_____

_____

Some amazing things that happened today...

_____

_____

What could I have done to make today even better?

_____

_____

Date: _____

Quote Of The Day

_____

_____

_____

Today I am truly grateful for...

_____

_____

_____

_____

_____

Here's what would make today great...

_____

_____

_____

_____

I am...

_____

_____

_____

Some amazing things that happened today...

_____

_____

Some amazing things that happened today...

_____

_____

_____

What could I have done to make today even better?

_____

_____

Date: _____

Quote Of The Day

_____

_____

Today I am truly grateful for...

_____

_____

_____

_____

Here's what would make today great...

_____

_____

_____

_____

I am...

_____

_____

_____

Some amazing things that happened today...

_____

_____

Some amazing things that happened today...

_____

_____

What could I have done to make today even better?

_____

Date: _____

Quote Of The Day

_____

_____

_____

Today I am truly grateful for...

_____

_____

_____

_____

_____

Here's what would make today great...

_____

_____

_____

_____

_____

I am...

_____

_____

_____

Some amazing things that happened today...

_____

_____

Some amazing things that happened today...

_____

_____

_____

What could I have done to make today even better?

_____

_____

Date:

Quote Of The Day

_____

_____

_____

Today I am truly grateful for...

_____

_____

_____

_____

_____

Here's what would make today great...

_____

_____

_____

_____

I am...

_____

_____

_____

Some amazing things that happened today...

_____

_____

Some amazing things that happened today...

_____

_____

What could I have done to make today even better?

_____

_____

Date: _____

Quote Of The Day

_____
_____
_____

Today I am truly grateful for...

_____
_____
_____
_____
_____

Here's what would make today great...

_____
_____
_____
_____
_____

I am...

_____
_____
_____

Some amazing things that happened today...

_____
_____

Some amazing things that happened today...

_____
_____

What could I have done to make today even better?

_____
_____

Date: _____

Quote Of The Day

_____

_____

Today I am truly grateful for...

_____

_____

_____

_____

Here's what would make today great...

_____

_____

_____

_____

I am...

_____

_____

_____

Some amazing things that happened today...

_____

_____

Some amazing things that happened today...

_____

_____

What could I have done to make today even better?

_____

_____

Date: _____

Quote Of The Day

_____
_____
_____

Today I am truly grateful for...

_____
_____
_____
_____
_____

Here's what would make today great...

_____
_____
_____
_____
_____

I am...

_____
_____
_____

Some amazing things that happened today...

_____
_____

Some amazing things that happened today...

_____
_____

What could I have done to make today even better?

_____
_____

Date: ☀

Quote Of The Day

_____

_____

_____

Today I am truly grateful for...

_____

_____

_____

_____

_____

Here's what would make today great...

_____

_____

_____

_____

I am...

_____

_____

_____

Some amazing things that happened today...

_____

_____

Some amazing things that happened today... ✨ ✨ 🌙

_____

_____

What could I have done to make today even better?

_____

Date:

Quote Of The Day

_____

_____

_____

Today I am truly grateful for...

_____

_____

_____

_____

_____

Here's what would make today great...

_____

_____

_____

_____

I am...

_____

_____

_____

Some amazing things that happened today...

_____

_____

Some amazing things that happened today...

_____

_____

_____

What could I have done to make today even better?

_____

_____

Date: _____

☀

Quote Of The Day

_____
_____
_____

Today I am truly grateful for...

_____
_____
_____
_____
_____

Here's what would make today great...

_____
_____
_____
_____
_____

I am...

_____
_____
_____

Some amazing things that happened today...

_____
_____

Some amazing things that happened today...   ✦ ✦ ✦ 🌙

_____
_____

What could I have done to make today even better?

_____
_____

Date:

Quote Of The Day

_____
_____
_____

Today I am truly grateful for...

_____
_____
_____
_____
_____

Here's what would make today great...

_____
_____
_____
_____
_____

I am...

_____
_____
_____

Some amazing things that happened today...

_____
_____
_____

Some amazing things that happened today...

_____
_____
_____

What could I have done to make today even better?

_____
_____

Date: _____

Quote Of The Day

_____

_____

_____

Today I am truly grateful for...

_____

_____

_____

_____

Here's what would make today great...

_____

_____

_____

_____

I am...

_____

_____

_____

Some amazing things that happened today...

_____

_____

Some amazing things that happened today...

_____

_____

What could I have done to make today even better?

_____

_____

Date:

Quote Of The Day

_____
_____
_____

Today I am truly grateful for...

_____
_____
_____
_____
_____

Here's what would make today great...

_____
_____
_____
_____
_____

I am...

_____
_____
_____

Some amazing things that happened today...

_____
_____
_____

Some amazing things that happened today...

_____
_____
_____

What could I have done to make today even better?

_____
_____

Date:

Quote Of The Day

_____

_____

Today I am truly grateful for...

_____

_____

_____

_____

Here's what would make today great...

_____

_____

_____

_____

I am...

_____

_____

_____

Some amazing things that happened today...

_____

_____

Some amazing things that happened today...

_____

_____

_____

What could I have done to make today even better?

_____

_____

Date: _____

Quote Of The Day

_____

_____

_____

Today I am truly grateful for...

_____

_____

_____

_____

_____

Here's what would make today great...

_____

_____

_____

_____

_____

I am...

_____

_____

_____

Some amazing things that happened today...

_____

_____

Some amazing things that happened today...

_____

_____

What could I have done to make today even better?

_____

_____

Date:

Quote Of The Day

_____

_____

_____

Today I am truly grateful for...

_____

_____

_____

_____

_____

Here's what would make today great...

_____

_____

_____

_____

I am...

_____

_____

_____

Some amazing things that happened today...

_____

_____

Some amazing things that happened today...

_____

_____

What could I have done to make today even better?

_____

_____

Date:

Quote Of The Day

_____

_____

_____

Today I am truly grateful for...

_____

_____

_____

_____

_____

Here's what would make today great...

_____

_____

_____

_____

_____

I am...

_____

_____

_____

Some amazing things that happened today...

_____

_____

Some amazing things that happened today...

_____

_____

_____

What could I have done to make today even better?

_____

_____

Date:

Quote Of The Day

_____

_____

Today I am truly grateful for...

_____

_____

_____

_____

Here's what would make today great...

_____

_____

_____

_____

I am...

_____

_____

_____

Some amazing things that happened today...

_____

_____

Some amazing things that happened today...

_____

_____

What could I have done to make today even better?

_____

Date:

Quote Of The Day

_____
_____
_____

Today I am truly grateful for...

_____
_____
_____
_____
_____

Here's what would make today great...

_____
_____
_____
_____

I am...

_____
_____
_____

Some amazing things that happened today...

_____
_____

Some amazing things that happened today...

_____
_____

What could I have done to make today even better?

_____
_____

Date:

Quote Of The Day

_____

_____

Today I am truly grateful for...

_____

_____

_____

_____

Here's what would make today great...

_____

_____

_____

_____

I am...

_____

_____

_____

Some amazing things that happened today...

_____

_____

Some amazing things that happened today...

_____

_____

What could I have done to make today even better?

_____

Date: _____

Quote Of The Day

_____
_____
_____

Today I am truly grateful for...

_____
_____
_____
_____
_____

Here's what would make today great...

_____
_____
_____
_____
_____

I am...

_____
_____
_____

Some amazing things that happened today...

_____
_____

Some amazing things that happened today...

_____
_____
_____

What could I have done to make today even better?

_____
_____

Date:

Quote Of The Day

_____

_____

_____

Today I am truly grateful for...

_____

_____

_____

_____

_____

Here's what would make today great...

_____

_____

_____

_____

I am...

_____

_____

_____

Some amazing things that happened today...

_____

_____

Some amazing things that happened today...

_____

_____

What could I have done to make today even better?

_____

_____

Date: _____

Quote Of The Day

_____

_____

Today I am truly grateful for...

_____

_____

_____

_____

_____

Here's what would make today great...

_____

_____

_____

_____

I am...

_____

_____

_____

Some amazing things that happened today...

_____

_____

Some amazing things that happened today...

_____

_____

What could I have done to make today even better?

_____

_____

Date: _____

Quote Of The Day

_____

_____

Today I am truly grateful for...

_____

_____

_____

_____

Here's what would make today great...

_____

_____

_____

_____

I am...

_____

_____

_____

Some amazing things that happened today...

_____

_____

Some amazing things that happened today...

_____

_____

What could I have done to make today even better?

_____

_____

Date: _____

Quote Of The Day
_____
_____
_____

Today I am truly grateful for...
_____
_____
_____
_____
_____

Here's what would make today great...
_____
_____
_____
_____
_____

I am...
_____
_____
_____

Some amazing things that happened today...
_____
_____

Some amazing things that happened today...
_____
_____

What could I have done to make today even better?
_____
_____

Date: _____

Quote Of The Day
_____
_____

Today I am truly grateful for...
_____
_____
_____
_____

Here's what would make today great...
_____
_____
_____
_____

I am...
_____
_____
_____

Some amazing things that happened today...
_____
_____

Some amazing things that happened today...
_____
_____

What could I have done to make today even better?
_____

Date: _____

Quote Of The Day

_____

_____

Today I am truly grateful for...

_____

_____

_____

_____

Here's what would make today great...

_____

_____

_____

_____

I am...

_____

_____

_____

Some amazing things that happened today...

_____

_____

Some amazing things that happened today...

_____

_____

What could I have done to make today even better?

_____

_____

Date:

Quote Of The Day

_____

_____

Today I am truly grateful for...

_____

_____

_____

_____

_____

Here's what would make today great...

_____

_____

_____

_____

_____

I am...

_____

_____

_____

Some amazing things that happened today...

_____

_____

_____

Some amazing things that happened today...

_____

_____

What could I have done to make today even better?

_____

_____

Date: _____

Quote Of The Day
_____
_____
_____

Today I am truly grateful for...
_____
_____
_____
_____
_____

Here's what would make today great...
_____
_____
_____
_____
_____

I am...
_____
_____
_____

Some amazing things that happened today...
_____
_____

Some amazing things that happened today...
_____
_____

What could I have done to make today even better?
_____
_____

Date:

Quote Of The Day

_____

_____

_____

Today I am truly grateful for...

_____

_____

_____

_____

Here's what would make today great...

_____

_____

_____

_____

I am...

_____

_____

_____

Some amazing things that happened today...

_____

_____

Some amazing things that happened today...

_____

_____

What could I have done to make today even better?

_____

_____

Date: _____

Quote Of The Day
_____
_____
_____

Today I am truly grateful for...
_____
_____
_____
_____
_____

Here's what would make today great...
_____
_____
_____
_____

I am...
_____
_____
_____

Some amazing things that happened today...
_____
_____

Some amazing things that happened today...
_____
_____

What could I have done to make today even better?
_____
_____

Date: _____

Quote Of The Day

_____

_____

Today I am truly grateful for...

_____

_____

_____

_____

_____

Here's what would make today great...

_____

_____

_____

_____

_____

I am...

_____

_____

_____

Some amazing things that happened today...

_____

_____

Some amazing things that happened today...

_____

_____

What could I have done to make today even better?

_____

_____

Date: _____

Quote Of The Day

_____
_____
_____

Today I am truly grateful for...

_____
_____
_____
_____
_____

Here's what would make today great...

_____
_____
_____
_____

I am...

_____
_____
_____

Some amazing things that happened today...

_____
_____

Some amazing things that happened today...

_____
_____

What could I have done to make today even better?

_____
_____

Date:

Quote Of The Day

_____

_____

Today I am truly grateful for...

_____

_____

_____

_____

Here's what would make today great...

_____

_____

_____

I am...

_____

_____

Some amazing things that happened today...

_____

_____

Some amazing things that happened today...

_____

_____

What could I have done to make today even better?

_____

_____

Date: _____

Quote Of The Day

_____

_____

_____

Today I am truly grateful for...

_____

_____

_____

_____

_____

Here's what would make today great...

_____

_____

_____

_____

_____

I am...

_____

_____

_____

Some amazing things that happened today...

_____

_____

Some amazing things that happened today...

_____

_____

What could I have done to make today even better?

_____

_____

Date:

☀

Quote Of The Day

_____

_____

Today I am truly grateful for...

_____

_____

_____

_____

Here's what would make today great...

_____

_____

_____

_____

I am...

_____

_____

_____

Some amazing things that happened today...

_____

_____

Some amazing things that happened today...

_____

_____

What could I have done to make today even better?

_____

_____

Date:

Quote Of The Day

_____
_____
_____

Today I am truly grateful for...

_____
_____
_____
_____
_____

Here's what would make today great...

_____
_____
_____
_____
_____

I am...

_____
_____
_____

Some amazing things that happened today...

_____
_____

Some amazing things that happened today...

_____
_____

What could I have done to make today even better?

_____
_____

Date:

Quote Of The Day

_____

_____

Today I am truly grateful for...

_____

_____

_____

_____

Here's what would make today great...

_____

_____

_____

_____

I am...

_____

_____

_____

Some amazing things that happened today...

_____

_____

Some amazing things that happened today...

_____

_____

What could I have done to make today even better?

_____

_____

Date: _____

Quote Of The Day

_____

_____

Today I am truly grateful for...

_____

_____

_____

_____

Here's what would make today great...

_____

_____

_____

_____

I am...

_____

_____

Some amazing things that happened today...

_____

_____

Some amazing things that happened today...

_____

_____

What could I have done to make today even better?

_____

Date: _____

Quote Of The Day

_____
_____
_____

Today I am truly grateful for...

_____
_____
_____
_____
_____

Here's what would make today great...

_____
_____
_____
_____
_____

I am...

_____
_____
_____

Some amazing things that happened today...

_____
_____

Some amazing things that happened today...

_____
_____

What could I have done to make today even better?

_____
_____

Date: _____

Quote Of The Day

_____

_____

Today I am truly grateful for...

_____

_____

_____

_____

_____

Here's what would make today great...

_____

_____

_____

_____

I am...

_____

_____

_____

Some amazing things that happened today...

_____

_____

Some amazing things that happened today...

_____

_____

What could I have done to make today even better?

_____

_____

Date: _____

☀

Quote Of The Day

_____

_____

Today I am truly grateful for...

_____

_____

_____

_____

Here's what would make today great...

_____

_____

_____

_____

I am...

_____

_____

_____

Some amazing things that happened today...

_____

_____

Some amazing things that happened today...

_____

_____

What could I have done to make today even better?

_____

_____

Date:

Quote Of The Day
_____
_____
_____

Today I am truly grateful for...
_____
_____
_____
_____
_____
_____

Here's what would make today great...
_____
_____
_____
_____
_____

I am...
_____
_____
_____

Some amazing things that happened today...
_____
_____

Some amazing things that happened today...
_____
_____

What could I have done to make today even better?
_____
_____

Date:

Quote Of The Day

_____

_____

Today I am truly grateful for...

_____

_____

_____

_____

Here's what would make today great...

_____

_____

_____

_____

I am...

_____

_____

_____

Some amazing things that happened today...

_____

_____

Some amazing things that happened today...

_____

_____

What could I have done to make today even better?

_____

_____

Date:

Quote Of The Day

_____

_____

_____

Today I am truly grateful for...

_____

_____

_____

_____

_____

Here's what would make today great...

_____

_____

_____

_____

I am...

_____

_____

_____

Some amazing things that happened today...

_____

_____

Some amazing things that happened today...

_____

_____

What could I have done to make today even better?

_____

_____

Date:

Quote Of The Day

_____

_____

Today I am truly grateful for...

_____

_____

_____

_____

Here's what would make today great...

_____

_____

_____

_____

I am...

_____

_____

_____

Some amazing things that happened today...

_____

_____

Some amazing things that happened today...

_____

_____

What could I have done to make today even better?

_____

_____

Date: _____

Quote Of The Day

_____

_____

_____

Today I am truly grateful for...

_____

_____

_____

_____

_____

Here's what would make today great...

_____

_____

_____

_____

I am...

_____

_____

_____

Some amazing things that happened today...

_____

_____

Some amazing things that happened today...

_____

_____

_____

What could I have done to make today even better?

_____

_____

Date: _____

Quote Of The Day

_____

_____

Today I am truly grateful for...

_____

_____

_____

_____

Here's what would make today great...

_____

_____

_____

I am...

_____

_____

Some amazing things that happened today...

_____

_____

Some amazing things that happened today...

_____

_____

What could I have done to make today even better?

_____

_____

Date: _____

Quote Of The Day

_____
_____
_____

Today I am truly grateful for...

_____
_____
_____
_____
_____

Here's what would make today great...

_____
_____
_____
_____
_____

I am...

_____
_____
_____

Some amazing things that happened today...

_____
_____

Some amazing things that happened today...

_____
_____

What could I have done to make today even better?

_____
_____

Date: _____

Quote Of The Day

_____

_____

Today I am truly grateful for...

_____

_____

_____

_____

_____

Here's what would make today great...

_____

_____

_____

_____

I am...

_____

_____

_____

Some amazing things that happened today...

_____

_____

Some amazing things that happened today...

_____

_____

What could I have done to make today even better?

_____

_____

Date: _____

Quote Of The Day
_____
_____
_____

Today I am truly grateful for...
_____
_____
_____
_____
_____

Here's what would make today great...
_____
_____
_____
_____

I am...
_____
_____
_____

Some amazing things that happened today...
_____
_____

Some amazing things that happened today...
_____
_____

What could I have done to make today even better?
_____
_____

Date:

Quote Of The Day

_____

_____

Today I am truly grateful for...

_____

_____

_____

_____

_____

Here's what would make today great...

_____

_____

_____

_____

_____

I am...

_____

_____

_____

Some amazing things that happened today...

_____

_____

Some amazing things that happened today...

_____

_____

What could I have done to make today even better?

_____

_____

Date: _____

Quote Of The Day

_____
_____

Today I am truly grateful for...

_____
_____
_____
_____
_____

Here's what would make today great...

_____
_____
_____
_____

I am...

_____
_____
_____

Some amazing things that happened today...

_____
_____

Some amazing things that happened today...

_____
_____

What could I have done to make today even better?

_____
_____

Gratitude for teens:

with prompts

Gratitude makes life better. Every day

is a new beginning.

I hope this journal has been useful to

you.

It would be great if you could leave a

review thank you.

ISBN: 9781096092230

www.ingramcontent.com/pod-product-compliance
Lightning Source LLC
Chambersburg PA
CBHW051352280526
45784CB00007B/2925